A Legacy of Liberty

THE FOUNDERS' VISION FOR THE ACTON INSTITUTE

A Legacy of Liberty
THE FOUNDERS' VISION FOR THE ACTON INSTITUTE

Robert A. Sirico

Introduction by Kris Mauren

ACTONINSTITUTE

A Legacy of Liberty: The Founders' Vision for the Acton Institute

© 2021 by Acton Institute

Originally published in 1997 and 2001 as *Toward a Free and Virtuous Society* and *The Entrepreneurial Vocation*.

Reissued with a new introduction in a combined edition as *A Legacy of Liberty: The Founders' Vision for the Acton Institute* by Acton Institute.

All rights reserved. No part of this publication may be reproduced, stored in a retrieval system, or transmitted in any form or by any means, including electronic, mechanical, photocopying, recording, or otherwise, without the prior permission of the publisher.

Scripture quotations marked (NRSV) are taken from the New Revised Standard Version Bible, copyright © 1989 the Division of Christian Education of the National Council of the Churches of Christ in the United States of America. Used by permission. All rights reserved.

Scripture quotations marked (KJV) are taken from the King James Version.

ISBN 978-0-578318-83-7 (paperback)
ISBN 978-1-880595-63-3 (ebook)

ActonInstitute

98 E. Fulton
Grand Rapids, Michigan 49503
616.454.3080
www.acton.org

Interior composition: Judy Schafer
Cover: Iron Light

Printed in the United States of America

Contents

Introduction by Kris Mauren	*vii*
Toward a Free and Virtuous Society	1
Notes	11
The Entrepreneurial Vocation	13
Stewardship of Talents: The Intellectual Divide between Religious Leaders and Entrepreneurs	15
The Practical Divide between Religious Leaders and Entrepreneurs	18
The Propriety of Moral Outrage	20
Entrepreneurs and Economists: Family Squabble or Sibling Rivalry?	22
Entrepreneurship as a Spiritual Vocation	27
Notes	37
About the Authors	45
The Acton Institute's Mission Statement	47
The Acton Institute's Core Principles	47

Introduction

Kris Mauren

Great things have small beginnings. When Fr. Robert Sirico and I co-founded the Acton Institute over thirty years ago, it was housed in a spare room in my apartment above a flower shop in Grand Rapids, Michigan. Now it has its own building in the heart of that city's downtown. Acton's mission of promoting a free and virtuous society characterized by individual liberty and sustained by religious principles began with conferences attended by dozens, and it continues with conferences attended by thousands from all over the world. This organic development mirrors Acton's vision of human flourishing, centered on the human person as the source and summit of both social institutions and economic life.

The human person may seem a strange focus for a think tank. Most endeavor to influence public policy, propose legislative initiatives, and attract the powerful. They are headquartered in state and national capitals, not midsized cities in America's Midwest. While Grand Rapids is remote from the powers and principalities of the world, it is a center of Christian publishing and scholarship fueled by its diverse and vibrant religious communities—Catholic, Reformed, and broadly evangelical. It is a center of both entrepreneurship and craftsmanship from furniture to beer. It works hard and prays hard, intuiting Lord

Acton's insight that, "Religion and political economy rule the world. That is, what men think best for them in this world and in the next."[1]

This simple insight is one that many either fail to notice or refuse to accept.

It is denied by materialists, cultured despisers of religion on both the political left—who claim that history is defined by class conflict—and the right—who view it as the product of a clash of civilizations or cultures indifferent to the universal character of human dignity. According to these materialist social visions, the interests of people are fundamentally antagonistic, while the truth, long ago articulated by the French economist and theorist Frédéric Bastiat, is that "men's impulses, when motivated by legitimate self-interest, fall into a harmonious social pattern."[2] Bastiat saw the materialist error promoted by both the socialists and liberal economists of his day,[3] and he posited that it requires a denial of the fundamental order of creation, countering, "I have complete faith in the wisdom of the laws of Providence, and for that reason I have faith in liberty."[4]

Critics of this vision of a fundamentally harmonious social order are also to be found among what Fr. Robert Sirico refers to in *Toward a Free and Virtuous Society* as "the political and ethical *cognoscenti*" of today, who "associate freedom with licentiousness, antinomianism, atomistic individualism, and a wide array of similar vices antithetical to virtue."[5] Among these critics are many sincere religious persons and in particular religious leaders. In his own day Bastiat described some such "Catholic" critics as claiming, "The great laws of Providence are hastening society along the road to disaster; we must escape them by renouncing worldly desires, taking refuge in self-abnegation, sacrifice, asceticism, and resignation."[6]

There is certainly some truth in this claim, for the apostle John instructs us all, "Do not love the world or the things in the world" (1 John 2:14 NRSV). At the same time, we are required to render service in the world to others (Matt. 25:35–

40). The economist and theologian Paul Heyne beautifully unpacked the implications of this duty in light of our human limitations:

> I do not know all that Christian love requires. But if it should require that we cooperate, through an extensive division of labor, in producing for one another food, clothing, shelter, medical care, prayer books, kneeling cushions, and other such material goods—then love requires that we interact extensively with one another on the basis of impersonal, monetary criteria.... Until we have transcended the human condition, we had better learn to cherish "the economy" and to nurture the conditions that are prerequisites for its successful functioning.[7]

The reality that land, labor, capital, competition, entrepreneurship—the whole of our exchanges and economic life—are fundamentally about service to others too often seems obscure, even to economists themselves! Economic life is about coordination of service in a world of limitations: "We cannot feel another person's wants; we cannot *feel* another person's satisfactions; but we can *render services* to one another."[8]

How should we serve one another with our God-given freedom and talents? What is freedom's relationship to virtue? These are the questions that Fr. Robert Sirico sought to explore in *Toward a Free and Virtuous Society* and *The Entrepreneurial Vocation*. These essays are represented here in a new combined edition *A Legacy of Liberty: The Founders' Vision for the Acton Institute*. They reflect our early efforts to explore these questions, grounded in an anthropology informed by Sacred Scriptures and natural law reasoning that puts the human person at its center. This assumes a capacity to know and approach the Truth of things with our reason, and the reality that we flourish in community and in harmonious relationships with one another. It also recognizes that we bring ourselves as individuals with due freedom in our actions and consciences into community.

At the end of the twentieth century, when half the world was dominated by communism and fascism, the human-centered approach of the Acton Institute to these questions was in many ways novel. Its namesake Lord Acton's nineteenth-century liberalism was decidedly out of fashion. Twentieth-century liberalism, right and left, increasingly wed itself to a progressivism far removed from the system of natural liberty espoused by Adam Smith, Edmund Burke, Frédéric Bastiat, and America's founders.

This progressivism sought to engineer society from the top down through broad-ranging economic and social reforms that often exacerbated the social and economic crises they intended to defuse. In the early twentieth century, movements such as the Social Gospel began to make headway in churches of all denominations, and the great Lutheran theologian Paul Tillich went so far as to say that "any serious Christian must be a socialist." By the late twentieth century, this progressivism even captured the imagination of churchmen, such as in the United States Catholic Bishops' 1986 document *Economic Justice for All: Pastoral Letter on Catholic Social Teaching and the U.S. Economy*. The letter included a whole host of specific economic policy recommendations, including fiscal and monetary policy, employment, minimum wage, taxation, education, welfare, agriculture, and international trade and aid, to name a few. While the bishops acknowledged that their recommendations on specific policy issues did not carry dogmatic weight and that they welcomed good faith debate on these issues,[9] the overlap with secular progressivism indicated (perhaps unwitting) ideological capture.

Anticipating much of the tenor of *Economic Justice for All*, in 1984 the Lay Commission on Catholic Social Teaching and the U.S. Economy by contrast issued the letter *Toward the Future: Catholic Social Thought and the U.S. Economy*. Like Bastiat, it advanced a providential theory of social coordination against the deterministic logic of central planning: "The Catholic understanding of God is ... as Providence, allowing contingent causes to work in all their baffling contingency, empowering human beings as free agents, compelling no one, but ordering all things sweetly and from their own proper natures and liberties."[10]

The Lay Commission's recommendations were less extensive than those of the bishops in *Economic Justice for All* and differed markedly in two distinct ways. First, the Lay Commission consistently placed the human person at the heart of its economic analysis, consistently reminding us that the economy is the *actions* of people and not simply an abstract force that *acts on* people. Second, it offered solutions not just to lawmakers in the form of public policy recommendations but also to individuals, families, communities, churches, and governments in their respective spheres of influence *within* the economy.

In this way it anticipated St. John Paul II's 1991 social encyclical *Centesimus Annus*, which analyzed, in the wake of communism's collapse in Eastern Europe, whether capitalism was the economic model most conducive to human flourishing:

> The answer is obviously complex. If by "capitalism" is meant an economic system which recognizes the fundamental and positive role of business, the market, private property and the resulting responsibility for the means of production, as well as free human creativity in the economic sector, then the answer is certainly in the affirmative.... But if by "capitalism" is meant a system in which freedom in the economic sector is not circumscribed within a strong juridical framework which places it at the service of human freedom in its totality, and which sees it as a particular aspect of that freedom, the core of which is ethical and religious, then the reply is certainly negative.[11]

The late theologian Michael Novak, Vice-Chairman of the Lay Commission and founding friend and advisor to the Acton Institute, foreshadowed and perhaps even greatly influenced this positive case for capitalism in his 1982 book *The Spirit of Democratic Capitalism*: "What do I mean by 'Democratic Capitalism'? I mean three systems in one: a predominantly market economy;

a polity respectful of the rights of the individual to life, liberty, and pursuit of happiness; and a system of cultural institutions moved by the ideals of liberty and justice for all."[12]

While the reductive and materialist conception of our economic life utilized by its would-be planners on both left and right represented a material misunderstanding, liberation theology fundamentally misunderstood the spiritual, and by extension social, dimension. One of the earliest and best-known liberation theologies—which developed in the Catholic Church in the context of post-colonial institutional failures, widespread poverty, and social injustice in Latin America during the late twentieth century—appropriated an anthropology of class conflict:

> Liberation theology is a method of defining Christian faith in a political context of underdevelopment, in a side-choosing spirit committed to action. It is no more concerned about the "working class" or "the poor" than Pope Leo XIII, whose 1891 encyclical underlined Catholicism's responsibility to these groups. Nor can it be universally defined as Marxist. Yet it gains its excitement from flirting with Marxist thought and speech, and from its hostility to the "North."[13]

Fr. Robert Sirico's first editorial in the *Wall Street Journal*, "The Sandinistas' Faithful Pilgrims," describes how the electoral defeat of the Sandinista regime in 1990 was unsurprising to him, having spent some time in Sandinista Nicaragua just prior to the election, but took both the mainstream secular and religious press by surprise. The charismatic priest and poet Ernesto Cardinal, the Sandinista Minister of Culture, had been the religious face of the brutal regime and had embraced a liberation theology wholly consistent with orthodox Marxism. Fr. Robert described how the regime captured the imaginations of many religious:

> "Turn to the classified section of most U.S. religious periodicals. You will find evidence of a cottage industry dedicated to sending North Americans to Central America to see for themselves the degree of support for the revolution."[14]

History does not repeat, but it certainly does rhyme. Liberation theologies have proliferated to include not just class consciousness and postcolonialism but black, feminist, womanist, and queer identity politics. All share an understanding of human relations as fundamentally antagonistic, ultimately grounded in abstract theories of power, rather than concrete human action and responsibility, guided by conscience, molded by religion, and oriented toward service to others in all avenues of life.

Given that we still face these ideological challenges today, albeit in new forms, the essays in this volume will still resonate with a modern readership. While the unflattering portrayals of entrepreneurs in the long-running television show *Dallas* may not be familiar to contemporary readers of these essays, they have a successor in *Succession*. The late twentieth century Christian Reconstruction movement in Reformed theology may have faded from prominence, but the critique herein of its confusion between the authority and power of the church is equally applicable to the contemporary resurgence of Catholic integralism. Today's bugbear of "Woke Capitalism" is examined in its earliest forms through the examples of Patagonia, Ben and Jerry's ice cream, and The Body Shop.

These challenges transcend the boundaries of creed and denomination. The Acton Institute's positive case for a free and virtuous society was always intended to be broadly multi-faith, and it is now more ecumenical than ever. While there is much resonance in our work from the Roman Catholic tradition (from the early modern Spanish Scholastics to Pope St. John Paul II), the Acton Institute has been a leader in *ressourcement* in Christian social thought within Protestant traditions as well. From early modern Protestant scholasticism to Abraham Kuyper's Neo-Calvinism, there is a rich Protestant tradition of meditation on the free and virtuous society. Judaism and Islam have their own such currents, too, and Acton has invested in scholars in those communities to further bring these sources to light and extend and develop lines of shared concern while being sensitive to fundamental differences.

Like all aspects of life affected by globalization, religious traditions often emerge enriched by encounters with other traditions and insights. The largest political party in the world, India's Bharatiya Janata Party, when it sought to define its ideology beyond Hindu identity, turned to the Catholic philosopher Jacques Maritain's Integral Humanism to distance itself from communalism and atomistic individualism and to articulate a vision of the good society rooted in natural law.[15] There is no singular vision of the free and virtuous society abstracted from the context of free and responsible individuals acting according to conscience rooted in religious principles.

Our task is, as the founder of the Paulist Fathers Isaac Hecker once said, to speak the "old truths in new forms." We ask, how can we return to first philosophy and recover public reason grounded in natural law? How can we engage in fruitful dialogue with persons with whom we may disagree over areas of common concern? How do we live lives of virtue in the context of the freedom upon which all genuine virtue depends? How do we contribute to social integration and solidarity in the face of social division? How can we reinvigorate the institutions of family, religion, business, community, and government, so vital to human flourishing? These questions were at the heart of the Acton Institute's founding and animate our pursuit of the free and virtuous society to this day.

At one of the very first conferences Acton hosted we had a remarkable participant. This Indian South African, committed Marxist, and anti-Apartheid activist was completely silent in the sessions focused on the human person, natural law, the economic way of thinking, and limited government. In the evenings after the sessions, we both engaged in spirited dialogue long into the night. Much of this sort of thinking about the free and virtuous society was completely new to him. He had many concerns and even more questions.

A month later I received a phone call from this man, thanking the Acton Institute for putting on the conference and introducing him to a whole host of new ideas. He then made a confession—ever since the conference he found political meetings unbearable. Having encountered Acton's vision of a free and virtuous society, he could no longer abide the reductionist conceptions of the human person, business, and the economy, or the antagonistic view of society uncritically expressed there.

This is our work. To plant the seeds of Lord Acton's vision of a "society that is beyond the state" and cultivate "the individual souls that are above it."[16] It has been a sincere privilege and one I am excited to continue. I would invite you, dear reader, to join us.

Notes

1. John D. Acton, "Add. Mss. 4870, p. 20," in idem, *Selected Writings of Lord Acton Volume III: Essays in Religion, Politics, and Morality*, ed. J. Rufus Fears (Indianapolis: Liberty Fund, 1988), 581.

2. Frédéric Bastiat, *Economic Harmonies*, trans. W. Hayden Boyers, ed. George B. de Huszar (Irving-on-Hudson: Foundation for Economic Education, 1964), xxi.

3. Frédéric Bastiat, *Economic Harmonies*, xxix.

4. Frédéric Bastiat, *Economic Harmonies*, xxx.

5. Robert A. Sirico, "Toward a Free and Virtuous Society," in *A Legacy of Liberty: The Founders' Vision for the Acton Institute* (Grand Rapids: Acton Institute), 1.

6. Frédéric Bastiat, *Economic Harmonies*, xxix.

7. Paul Heyne, "Christian Theological Perspectives on the Economy," in idem, *"Are Economists Basically Immoral?" and Other Essays on Economics, Ethics, and Religion*, ed. Geoffrey Brennan and A. M. C. Waterman (Indianapolis: Liberty Fund, 2008), 107-8.

8. Frédéric Bastiat, *Economic Harmonies*, 102.

9. United States Catholic Bishops, *Economic Justice for All: Pastoral Letter on Catholic Social Teaching and the U.S. Economy* (Washington: United States Catholic Conference, 1986), 68.

10. Lay Commission on Catholic Social Teaching and the U.S. Economy, *Toward the Future: Catholic Social Thought and the U.S. Economy, A Lay Letter* (New York: Lay Commission on Catholic Social Teaching and the U.S. Economy, 1984), 76.

11. John Paul II, Encyclical Letter on the Hundredth Anniversary of *Rerum Novarum, Centesimus Annus* (May 1, 1991), § 42.

12. Michael Novak, *The Spirit of Democratic Capitalism* (Lanham: Madison Books, 1991), 14.

13. Michael Novak, *Will It Liberate? Questions About Liberation Theology* (Mahwah: Paulist Press, 1986), 14.

14. Robert A. Sirico, "The Sandinistas' Faithful Pilgrims," *The Wall Street Journal*, March 13, 1990, A18.

15. Vinay Sitapati, *Jugalbandi: The BJP Before Modi* (Haryana: Viking, 2020), 54.

16. John D. Acton, "Add. Mss. 5011, p. 235," in idem, *Selected Writings of Lord Acton Volume III: Essays in Religion, Politics, and Morality*, ed. J. Rufus Fears (Indianapolis: Liberty Fund, 1988), 504.

Toward a Free and Virtuous Society

Freedom is, in truth, a sacred thing. There is only one thing else that better deserves the name: virtue. But then what is virtue if not the free choice of what is good?

—Alexis de Tocqueville

It is a telling commentary on our times that the political and ethical *cognoscenti* associate freedom with licentiousness, antinomianism, atomistic individualism, and a wide array of similar vices antithetical to virtue.[1] Despite this attitude on the part of many professional intellectuals, common sense tells any sane person that a society that is both free and virtuous is the place in which he or she would most want to live, but what exactly would it mean to advocate and work toward the construction of such a society? In what follows, I hope to offer a modest exploration of the notions of virtue and freedom and, to the extent that any limited examination allows, to analyze the ethical, economic, and practical premises upon which these noble notions rest. The purpose of this analysis is to establish a firm defense against the common objection that liberty is incompatible with virtue. Additionally, I will attempt to show that social structures characterized by liberty will best promote human progress and provide the context for the development of virtue.

One frequently hears the comment: "Liberty is fine, but it mustn't be taken to an extreme." According to this line of reasoning, liberty is only one virtue among many and should be balanced with numerous other virtues. The mistake here is that it is assumed that liberty or freedom is a virtue.[2] Now this is certainly an honest mistake, especially for those of us who live in the United States, where liberty is highly prized and embraced optimistically, but liberty should not be seen as a virtue in itself. Liberty is, rather, the context of actions and social institutions that facilitate or enable virtue. In other words, the requisite condition for a virtuous act is the ability to exercise choice in that action. We can thus say, then, that the predicate for virtue is liberty.

An animal cannot behave virtuously, because it lacks the faculty of reason; it is only the human capacity for reflection and purposeful action that enables man to act in a virtuous manner. Indeed, the exact opposite is true as well: No one can be said to be behaving viciously who does not have the capacity of moral reflection toward his actions. If conscious moral action is to have any virtue or vice, then free choice must be presupposed. Freedom therefore is closely linked to the nature of the human person, since free choice depends upon man's ability to reason. Any person who fails to employ his God-given capacity for reason is acting below his human potential. So, an understanding of the nature of the human person is fundamental to any discussion of man's freedom.

Broadly speaking, we might describe the human person as possessing both a physical and spiritual nature. Different religious traditions will describe these aspects of the person divergently, but each description must attempt to account for the tangible material components of the person, such as bones and hair, flesh and blood, and for the spiritual or transcendent reality of the human condition. This fact of transcendence may be expressed as the soul or spirit—that creative impulse that tugs us beyond the corporeality of our existence; that produces art, literature, music, and philosophy; and that, ideally, expresses itself in surrender to the call of God.

The Reverend Edmund Opitz, a Congregationalist minister who has been writing on these themes for many years, puts it this way: "Political theory in our tradition is based on the assumption that men must be free in society because each person has a destiny beyond society, which he can work out only under conditions of liberty."[3] If it is true that each individual has such a destiny, then he cannot be treated merely as a means to an end but as an end in himself. And if each individual is an end in himself, then it would be a gross violation of the essential nature and basic dignity that each person possesses to treat him as a means to someone else's ends. In addition to the violation of human dignity that would result, such a treatment of people (as means rather than ends in themselves) would undermine the very foundation of civil organization. No one, not even the perpetrator of human rights violations, ultimately would be safe in such a situation.

The human person is composed of material and spiritual aspects, but this juxtaposition does not imply a metaphysically schizophrenic entity. These two aspects of the human character make up the human reality: Human beings are flesh *and* spirit. We are not like angels who just happen to have bodies. We are not like beasts, who have no conscience. We are human beings: corporeal and spiritual.

The spiritual dimension of our character has to do with such things as honor, integrity, and so forth; indeed, many have sacrificed their physicality for the sake of these higher things.[4] The material dimension of our character pertains to the more mundane aspects of reality: material scarcity, property, economics, and the like. There is an interplay and mutual complementarity between the material and spiritual aspects of human existence.

Marriage clearly demonstrates, in a beautiful way, the interplay of the physical and the spiritual; this is most apparent when procreation is the result. Jacques Maritain calls the interplay of these distinct aspects the effort to distinguish in order to unite. This phenomena can also be seen in the social realm when, for example, personal liberty dovetails with economic liberty.

In many circles it is fashionable to defend personal liberties even when these are misconceived. For example, the ultimate right of singers to sing what they wish and of writers to write what they wish is rarely disputed in a liberal society, but when it comes to the right of traders to trade what they wish and buyers to buy what they wish, for some reason many view this as another matter altogether. Nonetheless, the connection between economic and personal liberties ought to be evident; it matters little to the writer to be told that he has the right to think and write as he wishes if he is not permitted to buy a typewriter or a computer, or if he does not have the right to sell his work freely to anyone who will buy it. The freedom to exchange information itself, such as in advertising—and, for that matter, in trading itself, which is really an exchange of information represented by an item's price—illustrates the connectedness of the personal and the economic, or the spiritual and physical realms of ultimate existence.

Additionally, the curtailment of economic liberty leads naturally to a curtailment of personal liberty in much the same way that the enhancement of economic liberty may lead to the enhancement of personal liberty.[5] Indeed, a cogent argument could be made that a significant reason for the collapse of communism in Eastern and Central Europe had to do with the communications revolution. Because devices like computers, facsimile machines, and even photocopiers make the exchange of information easier, it became necessary for totalitarian regimes to either permit a freer exchange of information or to become economically stagnant. This, in turn, made it considerably more difficult for totalitarian regimes to effectively control other kinds of information, such as political ideas and dissenting opinions.

Once it is established that liberty is the necessary context for virtue, it is important to delineate the appropriate and legitimate use of violence or coercion—that is, the threat of aggressive force—in society. It is my contention that physical violence of any kind may only be used to defend the rights of people and property, to enforce restitutionary sanctions for damages inflicted to people or property, or to satisfy the demands of justice, that is, by giving each his due. Everything else is best left to the noncoercive sphere as the first resort where additional and effective norms apply with mechanisms for adjudication and enforcement. The objection to employing violence for the sake of mere aggression stems from the nonaggression axiom, which simply states that physical aggression against person or property is morally wrong. This axiom plays a significant role in the political philosophy I am presenting. One great visionary of this political philosophy, Lord Acton, described it as follows: "Liberty is not a means to a higher political end. It is itself the highest political end."[6] Clearly, Lord Acton did not think that personal liberty is itself the highest end of man, and neither should we.

The question then arises, "How would social standards be maintained if people were free to disregard them?" In response, let us recall that Lord Acton's emphasis is upon *political* freedom, which is chiefly concerned with the legal use of aggressive force. Political freedom has nothing to do with "free love" or "free thought," nor does it call for freedom from "social authority" as exercised through the Church, workplace, family, and tradition.[7] Lord Acton's statement can be interpreted in the following manner: Insofar as people are concerned with the maintenance of political order, their primary focus should be upon the limitation of power and the advancement of human liberty. Human rights are first and best protected by strictly limiting the State's power of employing aggressive force; when the State is used for wealth redistribution, unjust wars, inflation, and the general regulation of the economy, such actions violate Lord Acton's dictum about the political order. This is why it is essential to maintain a distinction between society and the State, between voluntary and coercive institutions, and between authority and power.[8]

We want to acknowledge that Acton's claim, "Liberty is the highest political end of man," may appeal to a wide variety of philosophical foundations. For example, it may be grounded in radical skepticism, utilitarianism, hedonism, Kantian *a priorism*, Aristotelian natural rights, or in the Thomistic concern for the common good. In my thinking, some philosophical frameworks provide a more secure moral foundation for liberty than others. Hedonism, for example, provides no sound basis for a good society or a free market, even if the choice to act in this manner is voluntarily adopted. A free society with free markets does not necessarily result in the kingdom of God on earth. But then again, a free society does not pretend to be utopian. If the advocates of free markets in a free society were to wrongly identify the City of God with the City of Man, they would make the same error that Christian socialists of various stripes—from the social gospel movement through today's recently deceased liberation theology—have committed. Advocates of a free society may not allege, either for it or the free market, more than they are designed to accomplish. On this point, Opitz's analysis is once again helpful:

> The market will exhibit every shortcoming men exhibit in their thinking and peaceful acting, for—in the broadest sense—it is nothing else but that.... Catalog human shortcomings and you have compiled a list of the weaknesses and limitations of the market.[9]

This is why it is essential to emphasize that the market is necessary but not sufficient, that something more than economic liberty is essential for the establishment of a free and virtuous society, and that an economic calculus does not in itself give us the good.

The facts of scarce resources, human frailty, and the problem of original sin are each part of our existential condition from which only the kingdom of God can deliver us. Freedom alone can make no such claim; but what it can do, indeed, what history attests that the freedom of exchange has accomplished with remarkable proficiency, is maximize human resources to the greatest general benefit of humankind. The obligation of the State, then, is to secure, protect, and enforce the rights of individuals to maximize their creative potential. Alexis de Tocqueville wrote, "The idea of rights is nothing but the conception of virtue applied to the world of politics."[10] Beyond that, the promotion of virtue is best left to the province of natural society, that is, done within the spheres of authority of the Church, the family, the community, and at the demands of tradition.

The free market, as any entrepreneur knows, can function from time to time as a moral tutor by fostering rule-keeping, honesty, respect for others, and courage.[11] To function effectively, markets require a certain moral context and perspective on the part of entrepreneurs who participate in market activities. What business could long exist without a reputation for honesty, quality workmanship, civility, and courtesy? For, if a firm establishes a reputation for abusing its customers, people will cease to do their business there; in a market system based upon the principle of voluntary exchange, consumers have the freedom to refuse to do business with such firms.

The practical intelligence displayed in market activity is only its most obvious virtue; this can be seen both in the consumer looking for a good deal, as well as in the businessperson who must take note of others' interest by tending to the needs and desires of the consumer. In this respect, the system in which the entrepreneur must operate promotes what George Gilder has called altruistic behavior.[12] In a free market system, people succeed not by oppressing their neighbors but by serving them. Though certain unscrupulous individuals do take advantage of others, such behavior is anathema to the principles of the free society, which forbid force and fraud. In a truly free economic system, we do not exploit each other in our economic transactions. Rather, the opposite is true; we are given the opportunity to serve each other.

Voluntary institutions and the market are more trustworthy and effective than the State in the promotion of traditions, manners, ethics, and virtue. Michael Novak superbly describes the manner in which the market encourages effective laws and traditions that bolster virtue and social cohesion. He writes,

> In every culture, and in every market within it, there are special rules and traditions, sometimes tacit, which an apprentice needs time to learn. Such rules govern the range of bargaining discretion; the legitimate range of "mark-up"; the proper limits of disclosure; the acceptable standard of quality; the manner of conduct suitable to the transaction; considerations of time; systems of accounting; rights to return goods; arrangements for credit; and every other aspect of trade.[13]

These matters are too important to be entrusted to bureaucrats and politicians. It is not social authority to which I object but to coercive power, especially when it becomes centralized, as it has a tendency to do. No, authority ought to rest instead in a society's intermediary institutions—those social arrangements of authority that provide a buffer between the individual and the State. Furthermore, to the extent that the State intervenes into these institutions, society's moral fabric is weakened. The noted sociologist Robert Nisbet writes, "Only because of the restraining and guiding effects of such authority does it become possible for human beings to sustain so liberal a political government as that which the Founding Fathers designed in this country."[14]

It might be argued that it is counterintuitive to believe that human beings left free of constraint to follow their own choices and goals will cooperate with one another in such a way as to produce a cohesive social system. Some will, no doubt, argue that when such "*individualism*" is given free reign, the ties of the community will weaken and social structures will wane. The very word *individualism* is laden with such negative connotations, and we would do well to explore why this is so.

Each human person maintains an individual and distinct identity. Thoughts and emotions are experienced by the individual human mind. We are, even from the moment of conception, biologically distinct entities; though we abide within our mothers, we are not part of our mothers. Yet, to say that humans are individuals and in some sense autonomous, is not to contend that individuals are atomistic and isolated from the rest of the human family. We use language, which is a manifestly social behavior, and we come from families.

The insight of the French statesman Frederic Bastiat can help us grasp the fundamental unity between the social and individual dimensions of the human person. According to Bastiat, "Action flows from individuality, while the consequences overlap onto communities."[15] Moreover, "The whole of human society is made up of intertwined solidarities" that flow "from the communicating nature of intelligence."[16] Bastiat, virtually unknown to our contemporary culture, brings to the discussion of the relation between groups and individuals a keen and commonsensical approach. His most famous essay, *The Law*, anticipates some of the great economic questions that we grapple with today, and I believe that a renewed consideration of Bastiat's thought will enable us to clear away many popular misunderstandings. On the question of human community, or what a good nineteenth-century Frenchman would call "fraternity," Bastiat says, "It is impossible for me to separate the word *fraternity* from the word *voluntary*. I cannot possibly understand how fraternity can be *legally* enforced without liberty being *legally* destroyed, and thus justice being *legally* trampled underfoot."[17]

Bastiat saw how the various restrictions on human liberty resulted in hampering the development of community, what he called "human solidarity." This is most apparent in those restrictions affecting free trade, despite the moral intent of the legislators; such interventions interrupt the "diffusion of knowledge" that is essential if human resources are to be widely distributed and brought to the use of the human community. The advantages of a free society, Bastiat contended, "are hampered by the restricted system which tends to isolate peoples."[18] Thus, for Bastiat, it is liberty that most effectively promotes authentic human community, whereas "restriction," or what we today call interventionism, isolates people by dividing them into warring factions.

Our primary concern must not be whether people will become radically isolated from each other and turn into the much-denounced "atomistic individual," but rather, *which* community will people choose to join? Once this is answered, we may investigate the extent to which people will invest in any given community, and whether or not authentic solidarity will emerge from such relationships.

So the question turns on the kind of community that is appropriate to free, rational human beings. The alternatives are manifold: There is the community of the hive, in which individual dignity and rights are not given proper consideration. Alternatively, there is the community of the prison, in which human freedom, right of association—or nonassociation, for that matter—and individual creativity are not important. However, a community suitable for free individuals, which is progressive in the best and truest sense, and which encourages economically productive cooperation among its members, dramatically differs from the communities of the hive and the prison—it is what we call *civilization*.

In conclusion, I would like to note something that has become so apparent that to state it almost makes it redundant. Consider for a moment the events of the past few years. The colossal wreck of collectivism in Eastern and Central Europe—

and, we pray, one day soon in China and Cuba—as well as the decay and imminent collapse of the Western welfare states have permanently and irrevocably indicated the practical uselessness and moral bankruptcy of statism, that was and is, in Hayek's apt phrase, a "fatal conceit." The work that remains to be done is to clarify in our minds and in our spheres of influence that the choice of totalitarianism with virtue or liberty with vice represents a false dichotomy.

Liberty is indeed, as Lord Acton so elegantly puts it, "the delicate fruit of a mature civilization."[19] We can build, we must strive for, we cannot accept anything less than a society that is both free and virtuous.

Notes

1. For a related account of this lamentable state of affairs, see Paul Johnson, *Intellectuals* (New York: Harper & Row, 1988).

2. For the purpose of this discussion, I will use the terms *liberty* and *freedom* interchangeably.

3. Edmund A. Opitz, *Religion and Capitalism: Allies Not Enemies* (Irvington-on-Hudson: The Foundation for Economic Education, 1992), 93.

4. Ibid., 149–67.

5. See Milton Friedman, *Capitalism and Freedom* (Chicago: University of Chicago Press, 1964), 7–21.

6. John Emerich Edward Dalberg Acton, *The History of Freedom* (Grand Rapids: Acton Institute, 1993), 45.

7. See Friedrich A. von Hayek, "Religion and the Guardians of Tradition," in *The Fatal Conceit: The Errors of Socialism* (Chicago: University of Chicago Press, 1989) in which he makes the point that tradition is the cohesion that brings society into being.

8. Robert Nisbet, *The Quest for Community: A Study in the Ethics and Order of Freedom* (San Francisco: ICS Press, 1990), xxvi.

9. Opitz, *Religion and Capitalism*, 80.

10. Alexis de Tocqueville, *Democracy in America* (Garden City: Anchor Press, 1969), 237–38.

11. Michael A. Novak, *Free Persons and the Common Good* (Lanham: Madison Books, 1989), 13.

12. George Gilder, *Recapturing the Spirit of Enterprise* (San Fransisco: ICS Press, 1992).

13. Novak, *Free Persons and the Common Good*, 104.

14. Robert Nisbet, "Uneasy Cousins," in *Freedom and Virtue: The Conservative/ Libertarian Debate* (Lanham: The Intercollegiate Studies Institute, 1984), 20.

15. Frederic Bastiat, *Providence and Liberty* (Grand Rapids: Acton Institute, 1991), 45.

16. Ibid., 43.

17. Frederic Bastiat, *The Law* (Irvington-on-Hudson, NY: The Foundation for Economic Education, 1990), 25. Emphasis in the original.

18. Bastiat, *Providence and Liberty*, 46.

19. Acton, *The History of Freedom*, 21.

The Entrepreneurial Vocation

There was a time, in the not-too-distant past, when prejudice was an acceptable social posture. However, stereotypes, which typically function as shortcuts to knowledge, are today considered offensive. This is so, regardless of whether or not they elucidate a group characteristic. People ought not be judged merely by the associations they keep, without regard for their person or individual qualities. Such a tendency is objectionable to anyone with moral sensibilities.

Despite the laudable attitude of popular culture against prejudice of any form, there remains one group upon which an unfficial open season has been declared: entrepreneurs. One sees vivid evidence of this prejudice at nearly every turn, particularly in terms of popular forms of communication. Consider, for example, classic literary works (say, of Charles Dickens[1] or Sinclair Lewis[2]), television programs (such as *Dallas* or *Dynasty*), films (*The China Syndrome*, *Wall Street*, and some versions of *A Christmas Carol*), cartoon strips (such as *Doonesbury* and *Dilbert*), and even sermons in which entrepreneurs are depicted as greedy, immoral, and cutthroat.[3]

On the rare occasion when opinion makers, especially moral leaders, refrain from denouncing the "rapacious appetite" and the "obscene and conspicuous consumption" of these capitalists, about the best that one can expect is that business people be tolerated as a necessary evil. Most news editors, novelists, film producers, and clergy assume that commerce requires a broad and complicated network of controls to serve genuine human needs. Even friends of capitalism frequently display the same attitude. Religious leaders and critics of the market often suffer from confusion in their economic and moral thinking. This can be seen, for example, in their refusal to grant any moral sanction to the entrepreneur. Thus, instead of praising the entrepreneur as a person of ideas, an economic innovator, or a provider of capital, the average priest or minister thinks of people in business as carrying extra guilt. Why? For owning, controlling, or manipulating a disproportionate percentage of "society's" wealth.

While entrepreneurs should not be unfairly criticized for making money, they also must not be treated as victims of unjust discrimination who deserve a special blessing. However, it is also true that their chosen profession deserves to be legitimized by their faith. The public must begin to acknowledge the value of the entrepreneurial vocation, the wise stewardship of talents, and the tangible contributions of entrepreneurs to society.

The consequences of a divorce between the world of business and the world of faith would be disastrous in both arenas. For the world of business, it would mean not acknowledging any values higher than expediency, profit, and utility, which would result in what has been described as bloody or savage capitalism.[4] It would lead to a truncated view of consumers as well as of producers, whose sole value would be measured by utility. It does not require much imagination to gauge the effect such attitudes would exert on a wide range of social and civic norms. Similarly, the preconceived notions of religious leaders must be challenged to avoid the charge of "being so heavenly minded they are no earthly good." Forgetting that enterprise requires insight or intuition, and not merely a transcendent reference point directing it to the overall good of society, religious critics disregard the implicit spiritual dimension of enterprise.

Some moralists[5] seem to view business ethics as either an oxymoron or as an effort to subordinate what is intrinsically an ethically compromised mechanism to moral norms. To this way of thinking, ethics and business stand in fundamental tension with one another. However, I see matters differently. My work with an array of successful business leaders, extensive reading in the fields of economics and business ethics, and a fair amount of meditation and prayer on these matters have led me to the conclusion that *searching for excellence is the beginning of a search for God*. Put succinctly, the human thirst for the transcendent is what drives people to seek excellence, whether they acknowledge it or not. Nonetheless, this does not preclude our initial impulse and intuition from being a (divine) tug in the right direction. This is also the case with the human capacity for knowledge. Various philosophers and theologians contend that the human quest for knowledge reveals that human beings are ontologically oriented toward the truth. The human mind was originally designed to have an immediate awareness of the truth.[6] The principal argument of this essay is that the pursuit of excellence, like the mind's original constitution, discloses humanity's ontological orientation toward the highest and most supreme good, namely, the perfect apprehension of God in heaven (cf. 1 Cor. 13:12).

Stewardship of Talents: The Intellectual Divide between Religious Leaders and Entrepreneurs

The time has come for religious institutions and leaders to treat entrepreneurship as a worthy vocation, indeed, as a sacred calling. All lay people have a special role to play in the economy of salvation, sharing in the task of furthering the faith by using their talents in complementary ways. Every person created in the image of God has been given certain natural abilities that God desires to be cultivated and treated as good gifts. If the gift happens to be an inclination for business, stock trading, or investment banking, the religious community should not condemn the person merely on account of his or her profession.

In response to my writings in a variety of business journals, people of a particular profile contact me. On one occasion a gentleman called to let me know that he had just finished reading an article of mine in Forbes. It was, as he explained, both a shocking and emotional experience—shocking, because in all of his Roman Catholic school education and regular church attendance, he had never before heard a priest speak insightfully of the responsibilities, tensions, and risks inherent in running a business. Was there, he wondered, no spiritual component at all in what occupied so much of his life? In reading the article, he felt affirmed—for the first time—by a religious leader at the point in his life where he spent most of his time and effort: in the world of work.

This man represents many others whose stories are too numerous to recount here. Very often, they are relatively successful individuals with deep moral and religious convictions. However, each experiences a moral tension, not because what he or she does is somehow wrong, but because religious leadership has usually failed to grasp the dynamics of his or her vocation and thus provide relevant moral guidance and affirmation.

These people represent a variety of Christian traditions, and they all express a sense of being disenfranchised and alienated from their Churches. Religious leaders generally display very little understanding of the entrepreneurial vocation, of what it requires, and of what it contributes to society. Unfortunately, ignorance of the facts has not kept them from moralizing on economic matters and causing great harm to the spiritual development of business people. In particular, I recall one man, a self-described conservative Christian, saying that he no longer attended church services because he refused to sit in the pew with his family and, in effect, be chastised for his business acumen. How many critical sermons can a small-business owner or investment banker hear before he or she loses heart and decides to sleep in on the Sabbath?

Michael Novak relates another experience demonstrating the almost impenetrable resistance that some clergy exhibit to conceding the moral potential of market liberalism. His experience occurred at a conference on economics in which several Latin American priests were participating. The conference went on for several days, during which a persuasive case was made for how the free economy is capable of lifting the poor from poverty through the productive means of the market. The priests remained silent until the final day of the conference, and Novak offers an interesting account of what happened next:

> At the last session of what had been a happy seminar, one of the priests arose to say that his colleagues had assembled the night before and asked him to make a statement on their behalf. "We have," he said, "greatly enjoyed this week. We have learned a great deal. We see very well that capitalism is the most effective means of producing wealth, and even that it distributes wealth more broadly and more evenly than the economic systems we see in Latin America. But we still think that capitalism is an immoral system."[7]

Why does this state of affairs exist? Why is it so common that business people hear nothing better from a religious leader than something akin to, "Well, the way to redeem yourself is to give us your money"? Why is it that many of those who form the moral conscience of our world simply do not grasp either the moral foundation or basic principles of the market?

An obvious reason for this ignorance is the astonishing lack of any economics training in virtually all seminaries. It is rare to find a single seminary course explaining fundamental economic principles, the complicated world of stock trading, or microeconomic dynamics. Historically, in most social ethics courses, seminarians were accustomed to hearing the empty slogans of liberation theology proponents who believed that developed nations exploit less developed nations, thus keeping them in a perpetual state of poverty.[8] Generally, these arguments were put forth by theologians who had little grasp of economics.

The Practical Divide between Religious Leaders and Entrepreneurs

In addition to an intellectual or academic gap, there is frequently a kind of practical divide between religious leaders and entrepreneurs in their understanding of market operations. This is because the two groups tend to operate from different worldviews and employ different models in their daily operations. Notice how these differences are typically manifested. On Sunday morning a collection basket is passed in most churches. On Monday the bills are paid, acts of charity attended to, and levies paid to denominational headquarters. However, when the collection regularly comes up short, making it difficult to pay the bills, most ministers will preach a sermon on the responsibility of stewardship. In the minds of many clergy, economic decisions resemble dividing up a pie into equal slices. In this view, wealth is seen as a static entity, which means that for someone with a small sliver to increase his or her share of the pie, someone else must necessarily receive a somewhat smaller piece. The "moral solution" that springs from this economic model is the redistribution of wealth, what might be called a "Robin Hood" morality.

Entrepreneurs operate from a very different understanding of money and wealth. They speak of "making" money, not of "collecting" it; of producing wealth, not of redistributing it. Entrepreneurs must consider the needs, wants, and desires of consumers, because the only way to meet their own needs peacefully—without relying on charity—is to offer something of value in exchange. These people, then, view the world of money as dynamic. In referring to the free market as dynamic, however, it is easy to get the impression that we are describing a place or an object. However, the market is actually a process—a series of choices made by independently acting persons who themselves place monetary values on goods and services. This process of assigning subjectively determined values is responsible for producing the "wealth of nations," a phrase that is typically associated with the title of Adam Smith's classic eighteenth-century work[9] but was actually first employed in the Book of Isaiah (60:5).[10] The creative view of economics taken by business people is also illustrated in Scripture.

Unfortunately, the preceding argument may be misconstrued as urging that religion adopt a bottom-line, profit-and-loss mentality with regard to its mission, but this would be a grave distortion. I agree that there is a significant place for the sharing of wealth and resources within Christian practice—indeed, a mandatory place. With their transcendent vision, communities of faith recognize that some matters cannot be placed within the limited calculus of economic exchange or evaluated solely in terms of money. It is equally true, however, that to maintain credibility in the world of business and finance, clergy must first understand the inner workings of the market economy, for only then will such moral guidance be helpful.

But there is another, if somewhat misleading, factor that contributes to the hostility toward capitalism that one frequently encounters in religious circles. Many religious leaders spend a great portion of their lives personally confronting the wretchedness of poverty. Poverty saddens and angers us, and we want to put an end to it. This sentiment is entirely proper, not to mention morally incumbent upon Christians. However, a problem develops when this sentiment is combined with the economic ignorance described above. When this happens, the just cry against poverty is converted into an illegitimate rage against wealth as such, as though the latter created the former. While this reaction is understandable, it is nevertheless ill-informed and can lead to overreactions. Persons who react in this way fail to acknowledge that the amelioration of poverty will be achieved only by producing wealth and protecting a free economy.

The Propriety of Moral Outrage

There is understandable moral resistance to the image of successful business enterprise if one presumes that the engine of such activity is animated by greed, acquisitiveness, selfishness, or pride. The issue is not that some entrepreneurs are greedy or proud but whether these character flaws are the *norm* for successful practitioners of enterprise. The intent here is not to gloss over the fact that there are serious temptations associated with wealth and success but to come to a more balanced assessment of the moral character of entrepreneurs.

For some reason, moral critics often focus on the personal gains of entrepreneurs—as if wealth itself is somehow unjust—but lose sight of the many personal risks shouldered by these individuals. Long before entrepreneurs see a return on their idea or investment, they must surrender their time and property to an unknown fate. They pay out wages even before they know whether their forecast has been accurate. They have no assurance of profit. When investments do return a profit, much of it is usually reinvested (and some of it goes to charities and religious institutions). Sometimes entrepreneurs make errors of judgment and miscalculations, and the business suffers financial loss. The nature of the vocation is such that entrepreneurs themselves must accept responsibility for their losses without shifting the burden onto the public. For the person with a true vocation to be an economic agent of change, he or she must remain vigilant, for economic conditions are always changing.

When an economic risk fails, religious professionals should consider if it is not better to encourage than to condemn. Or should economic losses suffered by capitalists be viewed as their just deserts? Why not make such occasions opportunities to extend sympathy or pastoral care instead? *Whether they win or lose, by putting themselves and their property on the line, entrepreneurs make the future a little more secure for the rest of us.*

What is unique about the institution of entrepreneurship is that it requires no third-party intervention either to establish or to maintain it. It requires no governmental program or governmental manuals. It does not require low-interest loans, special tax treatment, or public subsidies. It does not even require specialized education or a prestigious degree. Entrepreneurship is an institution that develops organically from human intelligence situated in the context of the natural order of liberty. Those with the talent, calling, and aptitude for economic creativity are compelled to enter the entrepreneurial vocation for the purpose of producing goods and services and providing jobs.

Truly, the gifts that entrepreneurs offer society at large are beyond anything either they or others can fully comprehend. *Entrepreneurs are the source of more social and spiritual good than is generally recognized.* This fact, however, does not gainsay a pastor's proper role of spiritual direction, addressing not only moral failures but also misplaced priorities, neglect of family, and inattention to spiritual development due to overwork. Clergy must remind everyone of the seriousness of sin and call them to virtue, which means they must likewise challenge entrepreneurs when they go astray. To be authentic, this spiritual direction must be grounded in an understanding of what Judaism and Christianity have traditionally understood as sin, not in some politically correct economic ideology masquerading as moral theology.

This is a difficult transition for many religious leaders to make, especially because their inherited moral framework for understanding economic productivity was developed in a precapitalist world. It is an arduous undertaking to translate and apply premodern Christian social teaching to the dynamic environment of a modern, post-agrarian, postindustrial, and now, post-Communist world. It is especially difficult because, while human nature does not change, the socioeconomic context in which human nature exists is radically different from those cultures and societies where the principles of moral theology were first developed.[11]

Entrepreneurs and Economists: Family Squabble or Sibling Rivalry?

Economic theory has long had difficulty coming to terms with the nature of entrepreneurship, probably because it does not fit well into the econometric equations and graphs that depict the economy as a large machine. Entrepreneurship is too human an endeavor to be understood by science alone. That is where religion can be helpful in reconciling such people to the life of faith. Religious leaders must seek to understand entrepreneurs and encourage them to use their gifts within the context of faith. Of course, with wealth comes responsibility, and Pope John Paul II insists that even the decision to invest has an inescapable moral dimension.[12] Yet, entrepreneurs, by taking risks, serving the public, and expanding the economic pie for everyone, can be counted among the greatest men and women of faith in the Church.

Anti-Capitalist Capitalists

Even more puzzling than the anti-capitalist bias among the clergy is the bias found among capitalists themselves. In misguided attempts to achieve a high level of "social responsibility" for their companies, some business leaders have succumbed to false views of the marketplace. While creating wealth for society through their successful businesses, they simultaneously support causes antithetical to economic growth, free enterprise, and human liberty. Why does the rhetoric of "corporate social responsibility" seem to have such an anti-capitalistic bias? In the mid-1990s it became increasingly apparent that otherwise successful chief executive officers were using their corporations to fund politically interventionist causes under the rubric of corporate social responsibility. This could be seen particularly in the cases of Patagonia, Ben and Jerry's ice cream, and The Body Shop cosmetics chain.

Yvon Chouinard is the founder of Patagonia, a successful producer of functional outdoor sports clothing. Chouinard told the *Los Angeles Times* that he can "sit down one-on-one with the president of any company, anytime, anywhere, and convince [him or her] that growth is evil." His words, in fact, match his actions. In 1991 the company sent a letter to its dealers, announcing that it was "curtailing domestic growth" for economic and moral reasons. "We've taken a public stand in favor of more rational consumption in order to benefit the environment," the statement read. But, as *Los Angeles Times* reporter Kenneth Bodenstein relates, the situation in 1991 was quite different from Chouinard's public statements. It turns out that Patagonia had not "curtailed domestic growth" to maintain a high standard of social responsibility. "The company actually fired thirty percent of its staff, not because [it] was in deep financial trouble but because Yvon Chouinard's personal wealth was threatened." Interestingly, in Bodenstein's appraisal, Patagonia's situation resulted from ill-informed economic decisions such as Chouinard having "surrounded himself with managers with too little experience."[13]

Patagonia is, indeed, an unusual company. Chouinard donates one percent of Patagonia's total sales to environmental groups, including Earth First, an organization that gained notoriety for sabotaging logging machinery and infringing on private property rights. Patagonia also supports Planned Parenthood on the grounds that an increase in population threatens the future well-being of the planet. Chouinard desires his company to be a shining moral example to the corporate world. "If we can take the radical end of it and show it is working for us, the more conservative companies will take that first step. And one day they will become good businesses, too," he quips.

Ice cream entrepreneurs Ben Cohen and Jerry Greenfield, of Ben and Jerry's fame, though enormously successful as entrepreneurs, promote burdensome environmental controls and advocate giving welfare recipients broader rights to the public purse. Cohen and Greenfield have been leaders in the movement to restrict the production of bovine growth hormone, a drug that, when injected into cows, can increase milk output by up to 15 percent. They oppose the drug on economic grounds because they believe that it poses a threat to small-scale dairy farmers. However, the hormone, which was approved by the United States Food and Drug Administration on August 4, 1997, would also push down the price of milk, something that would be particularly helpful to poor families, if not to ice cream producers.

The Body Shop, the cosmetics chain with a naturalist bent, has been a vociferous supporter of animal rights and other left-wing causes. The company's founder and managing director, Anita Roddick, is a self-appointed preacher to the corporate world, chiding business people who are not "doing their share." "I am not talking about people who are just scraping up a living... I am talking about people who have huge, huge profits," she told the *Arizona Republic*. "You know, these CEOS with compensation packages bigger than the GNPS of some African countries."[14]

There are countless companies run by former 1960s-style radicals who try to reconcile their business success with the values of their youth. Everyone, business people included, has a right to advocate a chosen cause, as all customers have the right not to fund their causes by boycotting their products. But the pattern of these entrepreneurs displays an internal incoherence and suggests an attempt to do penance for capitalist "sins" that are not really sins at all.

These penitent capitalists castigate businesses that do not give enough back to society. A misplaced sense of guilt has clouded their understanding of how their own businesses do good for society, independently of social activism. Patagonia produces top-quality sporting goods. Ben and Jerry's serves up superior ice cream. The Body Shop sells inexpensive, all-natural cosmetics. Each of these companies brings satisfaction to millions and provides good products as well as jobs and investment opportunities. Their market success does not—and should not—need to be justified by support of anti-market causes.

The cynic might suggest that such postures are little more than marketing gimmicks. Socially aware chief executive officers such as Chouinard, Cohen, Greenfield, and Roddick have packaged 1960s idealism and are selling it for profit. When you buy a pint of Ben and Jerry's Rain Forest Crunch ice cream, you can feel good about helping save what used to be called "the jungle." The left-wing political slogans that adorn The Body Shop franchises are part of the image of cosmetics for the young and "socially aware." Such companies as Patagonia, Ben and Jerry's, and the Body Shop sell a mingled sense of moral superiority. These business people, using politically correct advertising slogans, can believe that despite their material success, they are giving something back to the world. Yet their "social responsibility" campaigns often become an irresponsible recipe for economic ruin.

These companies, and others like them, certainly profit from their association with left-wing causes. Meanwhile, taxpayers suffer from the advocacy of strict environmental controls, restrictions on FDA-approved growth hormones, and permissive attitudes toward sexual conduct. And would-be entrepreneurs are inhibited by new environmental regulations and welfare programs. We may commend business when it supports charities that lift people out of poverty, or purchases land to be preserved, or explores cures for diseases; *legitimate causes do not impede the market or push for more ill-conceived governmental action to solve social problems.* However, capitalism does not need more guilt-ridden leftists publicly flogging themselves and others for making money. Rather, capitalism needs more business people who understand that their greatest contribution lies in making profits, expanding jobs, boosting investment, increasing prosperity—and doing so in a way that promotes a wholesome, stable, and virtuous culture. *The proper moral response to capitalist success is both praise for the Creator who has provided the material world as a gift for all and also support of the economic system that allows prosperity to flourish.* Rather than doing needless penance, entrepreneurs such as Chouinard, Cohen, Greenfield, and Roddick should study fundamental economic theory—not to mention basic moral theology.

Dominion Theology and Economic Ideology

So far, we have discussed the aberrant "wealth-is-evil" branch of theological thinking held by so many clergy and even some entrepreneurs. However, there is a second branch that stems from the same root but takes an opposite approach. This is seen in what is called dominion theology or *Christian reconstruction*.[15] In response to liberation theology and the evangelical left, dominion theologians insist not only that the Bible provides the blueprint for structuring every aspect of society but also that as Christians attain a fuller understanding of the Bible, they will progressively take dominion over society, which will eventually usher in the kingdom of God. According to this theory, Christians will achieve global dominion, therefore, by voluntarily adopting the economic and sociological blueprint outlined in Scripture. Theonomist Gary North argues that applying these principles over time will naturally make Christians affluent, enabling them to procreate effectively and prolifically.[16] Thus, as Christians become increasingly affluent, numerous, and powerful, they will assume control of society. There is a natural correlation, it seems, between the theonomist's rationalization of personal affluence and the so-called prosperity gospel popular in Neo-Pentecostalism. Proponents of the prosperity gospel, also known as the health-and-wealth gospel, believe that God wants all Christians to be both healthy and wealthy and that there are certain "laws of prosperity" that, when applied correctly, inevitably produce these results.[17] Those who hold this view not only consider wealth as a sign of God's blessing but also intimate that economic hardship is a result of sin. Craig Gay pinpoints how dominion theology and the prosperity gospel coalesce:

> In a sense, then, dominion theology takes [the health and wealth] position several steps further, suggesting that individual aspirations to wealth fit into an eschatological framework that further legitimates them. From the perspective of Christian reconstructionism, the failure of Christians to become wealthy is not simply an indication of a lack of faith but actually postpones the coming of the kingdom of God.[18]

While dominion theologians correctly affirm the importance of free market economics, they also espouse an unbalanced and unbiblical view of the cultural mandate, creation theology, eschatology, and the reign of Christ. Such theological excesses might be curbed if partisans of both the left and the right were to consult (more frequently) the history of Christian thought for guidance in these matters.

Entrepreneurship as a Spiritual Vocation

Implicitly, and, at times, explicitly, faithful parishioners assume that the only real calling is to some kind of full-time Church work. In this view, lay people do not really have a vocation, though they do the best they can, given the circumstances. In 1891, canon law offered a simple but devastating definition of the lay person: "Lay: not clerical."[19] Since then, especially under the influence of the Second Vatican Council, a far more positive view has emerged, one that plumbs the depths of God's missionary objectives both inside and outside of the church.[20]

Looking at the gift of business acumen in an alternative way, however, enables us to grasp its spiritual and moral potential. An entrepreneur is someone who connects capital, labor, and material factors in order to produce a good or service. Michael Novak has argued that the entrepreneur's creativity is akin to God's creative activity in the first chapter of Genesis. In this sense, the entrepreneur participates in the original cultural mandate, given by God to Adam and Eve, to subdue the earth.[21] The entrepreneurial vocation is a sacred call similar to that of being a parent, even if it is not quite as sublime.

For several years, I have participated in programs designed to teach seminarians the importance of the free economy and the responsibilities of the entrepreneur. For many of these students, the ideas presented lead to eye-opening experiences. Students discover that the free market system is about creating wealth, about finding more effcient ways of serving others, and about providing people with jobs and investment opportunities. They discover that the chasm separating prosperity and morality is no longer insuperable.

In these seminars, I often mention George Gilder's extraordinary book *Wealth and Poverty*.[22] It can even be argued, I think, that Gilder is something of an intellectual entrepreneur. It is *Wealth and Poverty* that has been credited with being the intellectual force behind the 1980s' supply-side revolution, which forced economists and policy makers to consider for the first time how governmental policy, especially in the area of taxation, affects human choices. The popularity of this book illustrates well how someone outside academia can exert tremendous influence on American economic life. In my view, however, Gilder accomplished something much more important by insisting that *entrepreneurship is a morally legitimate profession.*

Gilder regards entrepreneurs as among the most misunderstood and underappreciated groups in society. As visionaries with practical instincts, entrepreneurs combine classical and Christian virtues to advance their own interests and those of society. Gilder thinks it is a mistake to associate capitalism with greed—an association with altruism would be far more accurate.[23] When people accept the challenge of an entrepreneurial vocation, they have implicitly decided to meet the needs of others through the goods or services they produce. If the entrepreneur's investments are to return a profit, the entrepreneur must be "other-directed." *Ultimately, business persons in a market economy simply cannot be both self-centered and successful.*[24]

The final chapter of *Wealth and Poverty* is perhaps the least read but most crucial of the entire book. Here Gilder presents the theory that entrepreneurship is an act of faith, an inescapably religious act.[25] By fusing traditional Christian morality with a celebration of growth and change, he helps us discern how knowledge and discovery are essential elements of enterprise.

Long before the publication of Gilder's Wealth and Poverty, an entire school of economics had grown up around Joseph Schumpeter's insight into entrepreneurship. According to Schumpeter, it was entrepreneurship—more than any other economic institution—that prevented economic and technological torpor from retarding economic growth. He thought that the function of entrepreneurs is

> to reform or revolutionize the pattern of production by exploiting an invention or, more generally, an untried technological possibility for producing a new commodity or producing an old one in a new way, by opening up a new source of supply of materials or a new outlet for products, by reorganizing an industry and so on.[26]

Entrepreneurs, as agents of change, encourage the economy to adjust to population increases, resource shifts, and changes in consumer needs and desires. Without entrepreneurs, we would face a static economic world not unlike the stagnant economic swamps that socialism brought about in central Europe.

The economic analysis that has its roots in Schumpeter's work taught that entrepreneurs are *impresarios*, visionaries who organize numerous factors, take risks, and combine resources to create something greater than the sum of its parts.[27] Entrepreneurs drive the economy forward by anticipating the wishes of the public and creating new ways of organizing resources. In short, they are men and women who create jobs, discover and apply new cures, bring food to those in need, and help dreams become realities.

The Biblical Case for Entrepreneurship

Those who consider the entrepreneurial vocation a necessary evil, who view profits with open hostility, should realize that Scripture lends ample support to entrepreneurial activity. The Bible teaches us eternal truths but also provides surprisingly practical lessons for worldly affairs. In Matthew 25:14–30, we find Jesus' parable of the talents. As with all parables, its meaning is multilayered. Its eternal meaning relates to how we use God's gift of grace. With regard to the material world, it is a story about capital, investment, entrepreneurship, and the proper use of economic resources. It is a direct rebuttal to those who insist that business success and Christian living are contradictory. What follows is the text of this parable with commentary that applies principles taken from the parable to the entrepreneurial vocation.

> For it is as if a man, going on a journey, summoned his slaves and entrusted his property to them; to one he gave five talents; to another, two; to another, one, to each according to his ability. Then he went away. The one who had received the five talents went off at once and traded with them, and made five more talents. In the same way, the one who had the two talents made two more talents. But the one who had received the one talent went off and dug a hole in the ground and hid his master's money. After a long time, the master of those slaves came and settled accounts with them. Then the one who had received the five talents came forward, bringing five more talents, saying, "Master, you handed over

to me five talents; see, I have made five more talents." His
master said to him, "Well done, good and trustworthy slave;
you have been trustworthy in a few things, I will put you in
charge of many things; enter into the joy of your master."
And the one with two talents also came forward, saying,
"Master, you handed over to me two talents; see, I have made
two more talents." His master said to him, "Well done, good
and trustworthy slave; you have been trustworthy in a few
things, I will put you in charge of many things; enter into
the joy of your master." Then the one who had received the
one talent also came forward, saying, "Master I knew that
you were a harsh man, reaping where you did not sow, and
gathering where you did not scatter seed; so I was afraid,
and I went and hid your talent in the ground. Here you have
what is yours." But his master replied, "You wicked and lazy
slave! You knew, did you, that I reap where I did not sow,
and gather where I did not scatter? Then you ought to have
invested my money with the bankers, and on my return I
would have received what was my own with interest. So
take the talent from him, and give it to the one with the
ten talents. For to all those who have, more will be given,
and they will have an abundance; but from those who have
nothing, even what they have will be taken away. As for this
worthless slave, throw him into the outer darkness, where
there will be weeping and gnashing of teeth."

—Matt. 25:14–30 NRSV

This is a story that many religious leaders do not often apply
to real life. When people think of Jesus' parables, the parable
of the talents is not usually the first to come to mind. Perhaps
this is because most religious leaders hold to an ethic where
profit is suspect and entrepreneurship is frowned upon. Yet the
preceding story relays an immediately apparent ethical meaning,
not to mention even deeper lessons for economic accountability
and proper stewardship.

The word *talent* in this parable has two meanings. First, it is a monetary unit, perhaps even the largest denomination of Jesus' time. The editors of the *New Bible Commentary* agree that a talent was a very large sum of money; in modern terms, it would have been equivalent to several thousand dollars.[28] So, we know that the amount given to each servant was considerable. Second, more broadly interpreted, the word *talent* refers to all of the various gifts God has given us to cultivate and multiply. This definition embraces all gifts, including our natural abilities and resources as well as our health, education, possessions, money, and opportunities.

I do not pretend to build an entire ethic for capitalism from this parable. To do so would be to commit an egregious exegetical and historical error, similar to those committed by liberation and dominion theologians. Yet, *one of the simplest lessons from this parable has to do with how we use our God-given capacities and resources*. This, I contend, must be part of an ethic that guides economic activity and decision-making in the marketplace. On one level, in the same way the master expected productive activity from his servants, God wants us to use our talents toward constructive ends. We see here that in setting off on his journey, the master allows his servants to decide upon the best manner of investment. In this regard, they have full liberty. In fact, the master does not even command them to invest profitably; instead, he merely assumes their goodwill and interest in his property. Given this implicit trust, it is easier to understand the master's eventual disgust with the unprofitable servant. It is not so much his lack of productivity that offends the master as the underlying attitude he exhibits toward the master and his property. One can imagine the servant's reasoning: "I'll just get by; I'll put this talent out of sight so that I don't have to deal with it, monitor it, or be accountable for it." One biblical scholar, Leopold Fonck, observes, "It is not the misuse only of the gifts received which renders the recipient guilty in the sight of God, but the non-use also."[29] The master invited each of the diligent servants to rejoice in his own joy, once they had shown themselves to be productive. They were handsomely rewarded; indeed, the master gave the lazy servant's single talent to the one who had been given ten.

The parable of the talents, however, presupposes a local understanding of the proper stewardship of money. According to rabbinical law, burying was regarded as the best security against theft. If a person entrusted with money buried it as soon as he took possession of it, he would be free from liability, should anything happen to it. For money merely tied up in a cloth, the opposite was true. In this case, the person was responsible to cover any loss incurred due to the irresponsible nature of the deposit.[30] Yet, in the parable of the talents, the master encourages reasonable risk-taking. He considers the act of burying the talent—and thus breaking even—to be foolish, because he believes capital should earn a reasonable rate of return. In this understanding, time is money (another way of discussing interest).

A second critical lesson from the parable is this: *It is not immoral to profit from our resources, wit, and labor.* Though writing for an entirely different audience and context, Austrian economist Israel Kirzner employs the concept of entrepreneurial alertness to show the significance of cultivating one's natural ability, time, and resources. Building on the work of Ludwig von Mises, Kirzner acknowledges that by seeking new opportunities and engaging in goal-directed activity, entrepreneurs strive "to pursue goals efficiently, once ends and means are clearly identified, but also with the drive and alertness needed to identify which ends to strive for and which means are available."[31] Without overstating the similarity between Kirzner's concept and the parable of the talents, there seems to be a natural connection between the discovery of entrepreneurial opportunities and the master's (the Lord's) admonition in Matthew 25 to be watchful of his return and to be caretakers of his property. Thus, with respect to profit, the only alternative is loss, which, in the case of the third servant, constitutes poor stewardship.[32] However, the voluntary surrender of wealth, such as in almsgiving or in its more radical form of renouncing the right to ownership of property (as in the traditional vow of poverty taken by members of certain religious orders),[33] should not be confused with economic loss. In the former case, a legitimate good is foregone in exchange for another to which one has been uniquely called. In the latter case, to fail deliberately in an economic endeavor, or to do so as a result of sloth, is to show disrespect for God's gift and for one's responsibility as a steward.

Nevertheless, we must distinguish properly between the moral obligations to be economically creative and productive, on the one hand, and to employ one's talents and resources prudently and magnanimously, on the other. It is clear from our discussion of the parable of the talents and the cultural mandate in Genesis 1 that in subduing the earth, people need to be attentive to the possibilities for change, development, and investment. Furthermore, because humans are created in the image of God and have been endowed with reason and free will, human actions necessarily involve a creative dimension. Thus, in the case of the third servant who placed his single talent into the ground, it was the nonuse of his ability to remain alert to future possibilities—which precluded any productive return on the master's money—that led to his being severely chastised.

There is, perhaps, no clearer illustration of employing one's talents and resources prudently for the good of all than the monks of the medieval Cistercian monasteries. Insofar as monasteries were ruled by a religious constitution that divided each monk's day into segments devoted to prayer, contemplation, worship, and work, the amount of time available to spend on productive activities was tightly regulated. This constraint, along with the typical monastic emphasis on self-sufficiency, motivated monasteries to develop more efficient farm-production techniques, which provided a natural incentive to embrace technological development. In addition to the early and frequent use of mills, Cistercian monks also experimented with plants, soils, and breeding stocks, thus enabling them to use their God-given creativity wisely and productively in order to accumulate money for the monastery and to aid the poor.[34]

Economics shows that the rate of return (profit) on capital over the long run is likely to equal the interest rate. The rate of interest, in turn, is the payment given for putting off present consumption for future consumption (sometimes called the rate of time preference). For the master in Jesus' parable, it was not enough merely to recover the original value of the talent; rather, he expected the servant to increase its value through participation in the economy. Even a minimal level of participation, such as keeping money in an interest-bearing account, would have yielded a small rate of return on the master's capital. Burying capital in the ground sacrifices even that minimal amount of return, which was what incensed the master about his servant's indolence.

In the book of Genesis, we read that God gave the earth with all its resources to Adam and Eve. Adam was to mix his labor with the raw material of creation to produce usable goods for his family.[35] Similarly, the master in the parable of the talents expected his servants to use the resources at their disposal to increase the value of his holdings. Rather than passively preserve what they had been given, the two faithful servants invested the money, but the master was justly angered at the timidity of the servant who had received one talent. Through this parable, God commands us to use our talents productively. Through this parable, we are exhorted to work, be creative, and reject idleness.

Throughout history, people have endeavored to construct institutions that ensure security and minimize risk—much as the failed servant tried to do with the master's money. Such efforts range from the Greco-Roman welfare States, to the Luddite communes of the 1960s, to full-scale Soviet totalitarianism. From time to time, these efforts have been embraced as "Christian" solutions to future insecurities. Yet, uncertainty is not just a hazard to be avoided; it can be an opportunity to glorify God through wise use of his gifts. In the parable of the talents, courage in the face of an unknown future was generously rewarded in the case of the first servant, who had been entrusted with the most. He used the five talents to acquire five more. It would have been safer for him to deposit the money in a bank and receive a nominal interest rate. For taking reasonable risks and displaying entrepreneurial acumen, he was allowed to retain his original allotment as well as his new earnings. Furthermore, he was even invited to rejoice with the master. The lazy servant could have avoided his dismal fate by demonstrating more entrepreneurial initiative. If he had made an effort to increase his master's holdings but failed in the process, he may not have been judged so harshly.

The parable of the talents implies a moral obligation to confront uncertainty in an enterprising way. There is no more apt example of such an individual than that of the entrepreneur. Entrepreneurs look to the future with courage and a sense of opportunity. In creating new enterprises, they open up new options for people with regard to earning a wage and developing their skills. But none of what has been argued should be taken to imply that the entrepreneur, because of the importance that he or she holds for society, should be exempted from spiritual accountability. Immoral behavior can be found among entrepreneurs no less often than among any other group of sinful human beings. However, *it is important neither to canonize poverty nor to demonize economic success.*

No doubt, in the pursuit of their vocation, business leaders will be tempted in many ways. Sometimes the temptation will be thinking that the humdrum world of business and finance is spiritually insignificant and that the bottom line is paramount. In such moments, entrepreneurs must reflect anew on the twenty-fifth chapter of Matthew's gospel and grasp the fact that God has entrusted them with their talents and that he expects entrepreneurs to be industrious, generous, and innovative with them. And if they will be faithful to this calling, they may hope to hear the words spoken by the Master to those first servants:

> Well done, thou good and faithful servant. Thou hast been faithful over a few things; I will make thee ruler over many things. Enter thou into the joy of thy Lord.
>
> —Matt. 25:21 KJV

Notes

1. Charles Dickens, *Hard Times for These Times* (London: Oxford University Press, 1955 [1854]); *Dealings with the Firm of Dombey and Son, Wholesale, Retail, and for Exportation* (London: Oxford University Press, 1964 [1847–1848]).

2. Sinclair Lewis, *Babbitt* (New York: Harcourt, Brace, and Company, 1922).

3. For a fuller description of how businesspeople have been depicted in literature, see Michael J. McTague, *The Businessman in Literature: Dante to Melville* (New York: Philosophical Library, 1979).

4. Ibid., 63–71.

5. The quintessential historical representative of this position would be Bernard Mandeville, who thought that economic prosperity resulted from the actions of self-seeking and amoral individuals. He argued that to achieve economic success, people must be liberated from the restraints of conventional morality. This relegated the prescriptions of business ethics to the status of useful fictions created to maintain order and ensure predictable results. *The Fable of the Bees*, vol. 1, ed. F. B. Kaye (London: Oxford University Press, 1924 [1705]), 46. For a criticism of Mandeville and his contemporary followers, see Norman P. Barry, *Anglo-American Capitalism and the Ethics of Business* (Wellington, New Zealand: New Zealand Business Roundtable, 1999), 8–16; also cf., Norman P. Barry, *The Morality of Business Enterprise* (Aberdeen: Aberdeen University Press, 1991), 3–6.

6. John Paul II, *Crossing the Threshold of Hope*, ed. Vittorio Messori (New York: Alfred A. Knopf, 1994), 32–36; Encyclical Letter *Fides et Ratio* (September 14, 1998), nos. 4–5, 27.

7. Michael Novak, *This Hemisphere of Liberty: A Philosophy of the Americas* (Washington: AEI Press, 1990), 38.

8. According to Gregory Baum, then professor of theology and religious studies at Saint Michael's College, University of Toronto:

   > [T]he economic dependence of the Latin American countries on the system of corporate capitalism, with its center in the North Atlantic community and more especially in the United States, has not only led to the impoverishment of the mass of the population in the city and country but also has affected the cultural and educational institutions and through them the consciousness of the people in general.

   The Social Imperative: Essays on the Critical Issues That Confront the Christian Churches (New York: Paulist Press, 1979), 10.

   Or, as Northwestern University professor Rosemary Ruether writes:

   > [I]t is only in Latin America that the real theology of liberation can be written, whereas Europeans and North Americans, who remain encompassed by their own status as beneficiaries of oppressive power, can only comment upon this theology from outside.

   Liberation Theology: Human Hope Confronts Christian History and American Power (New York: Paulist Press, 1972), 181.

   For a cogent critique of these approaches, see Michael Novak, *Will It Liberate? Questions About Liberation Theology* (New York: Paulist Press, 1986).

9. Adam Smith, *An Inquiry into the Nature and Causes of the Wealth of Nations*, ed. R. H. Campbell and A. S. Skinner (Oxford: Oxford University Press, 1976 [1776]).

10. The text of the verse reads (NRSV):

> Then you shall see and be radiant;
> > Your heart shall thrill and rejoice,
> because the abundance of the sea shall be brought to you,
> > the wealth of the nations shall come to you.

11. In the two years preceding his reception into the Roman Catholic Church (1843–1845), John Henry Cardinal Newman wrote his now-famous work, *An Essay on the Development of Christian Doctrine* (London: J. Toovey, 1845). Unfortunately, then as now, it is all too common that well-meaning and faithful Roman Catholics associate a growing Christian self-understanding and maturity in the area of doctrine and morals with a relativist worldview. It is true that some theologians are in jeopardy of slipping into relativism; however, to argue, as some do, that any doctrinal emendation will necessarily lead to relativism is false. In the case of Cardinal Newman, the main task of his essay was to examine the principal differences between doctrinal corruption and doctrinal development. In the essay, he insists that a true and fertile idea is endowed with a certain vital and assimilative energy of its own, which, without experiencing substantive change, attains a more complete expression as it encounters new aspects of truth or collides with new errors over time. Thus, Cardinal Newman employs an organic metaphor to describe how doctrinal ideas develop over the course of time through the Church's new experiences, discoveries, and revelations. To bolster his argument, he provides a series of tests for distinguishing true development from corruption, the chief of which are the preservation of type and the continuity of principles. It is important to grasp, therefore, that the essence of the doctrine—*both in its earlier and later forms*—was contained in the original revelation given to the church by Christ and the apostles, and guaranteed by its Magisterium.

12. John Paul II, Encyclical Letter *Centesimus Annus* (May 1, 1991), nos. 29, 32.

13. Kenneth Bodenstein, "Pure Profit: For Small Companies That Stress Social Values As Much As the Bottom Line, Growing Up Hasn't Been an Easy Task," *Los Angeles Times Magazine* (February 5, 1995): 4.

14. Jodie Snyder, "Social Awareness: Corporate America Cultivates Conscience," *Arizona Republic* (May 12, 1994): 6.

15. The principal representatives of dominion theology are: Gary North, Rousas J. Rushdoony, Greg Bahnsen, David Chilton, Rodney Clapp, and Gary DeMar.

16. Gary North, *Liberating Planet Earth: An Introduction to Biblical Blueprints* (Fort Worth: Dominion Press, 1987), 81.

17. See Bruce Barton, *The Health and Wealth Gospel* (Downers Grove: InterVarsity Press, 1987).

18. Craig M. Gay, *With Liberty and Justice for Whom? The Recent Evangelical Debate Over Capitalism* (Grand Rapids: Eerdmans, 1991), 103, ftn. 191. For an incisive exposition and critique of dominion theology, see pages 101–9.

19. See Yves Congar, OP, "The Laity," in *Vatican II: An Interfaith Appraisal* (Notre Dame: University of Notre Dame Press, 1966), 240.

20. *In Gaudium et Spes*, the Second Vatican Council promulgates a much more positive understanding of the role of the laity. In paragraph 43, the Council states:

    > Let Christians follow the example of Christ, who worked as a craftsman; let them be proud of the opportunity to carry out their earthly activity in such a way as to integrate human, domestic, professional, scientific, and technical enterprises with religious values, under whose supreme direction all things are ordered to the glory of God.
    >
    > It is to the laity, though not exclusively to them, that secular duties and activity properly belong. When, therefore, as citizens of the world, they are engaged in any activity either individually or collectively, they will not be satisfied with meeting the minimum legal requirements but will

strive to become truly proficient in that sphere.... It is to their task to cultivate a properly informed conscience and to impress the divine law on the affairs of the earthly city. For guidance and spiritual strength let them turn to the clergy but let them realize that their pastors will not always be so expert as to have a ready answer to every problem (even every grave problem) that arises; this is not the role of the clergy: It is, rather, up to the laymen to shoulder their responsibilities under the guidance of Christian wisdom and with eager attention to the teaching authority of the Church.

The laity are called to participate actively in the whole life of the Church; not only are they to animate the world with the spirit of Christianity, but they are to be witnesses to Christ in all circumstances and at the very heart of the community of mankind.

21. Michael Novak, *The Spirit of Democratic Capitalism* (New York: Simon and Schuster, 1982), 98.

22. George Gilder, *Wealth and Poverty*, rev. ed. (San Francisco: ICS Press, 1993).

23. Ibid., 21, 24.

24. Ibid., 28.

25. Ibid., 276–80.

26. Joseph A. Schumpeter, *Capitalism, Socialism, and Democracy*, 3rd ed. (New York: Harper and Brothers Publishers, 1950), 132.

27. Schumpeter provides the following apt description of the entrepreneur: "To act with confidence beyond the range of familiar beacons and to overcome ... resistance requires aptitudes that are present in only a small fraction of the population and that define the entrepreneurial type as well as the entrepreneurial function." Ibid.

28. G. J. Wenham, J. A. Motyer, D. A. Carson, and R. T. France, eds., *New Bible Commentary, Twenty-First Century Edition* (Downers Grove: InterVarsity Press, 1997), 938.

29. Leopold Fonck, *The Parables of the Gospel: An Exegetical and Practical Explanation*, 3d ed., ed. George O'Neill, trans. E. Leahy (New York: F. Pustet, 1914 [1902]), 542.

30. According to the teaching of Rabbi Gemara, "Samuel said: Money can only be guarded [by placing it] in the earth. Said Raba: Yet Samuel admits that on Sabbath eve at twilight the Rabbis did not put one to that trouble. Yet if he tarried after the conclusion of the Sabbath long enough to bury it [the money] but omitted to do so, he is responsible [if it is stolen]." *The Babylonian Talmud* (Seder Nezikin), *Baba Metzia*, vol. 1, trans. H. Freedman (New York: Rebecca Bennet Publications Inc., 1959), 250–51. Also see the very next section (254–59) for a detailed discussion of liability surrounding the deposit of money with a bailiff, private individual, or third party.

31. Israel M. Kirzner, *Competition and Entrepreneurship* (Chicago: University of Chicago Press, 1973), 33.

32. Kirzner points out that entrepreneurial responses to changes in information should not be understood as a process of calculation. Rather, the entrepreneurial dimension concerns that element of a decision involving "a shrewd and wise assessment of the realities (both present and future) within the context of which the decision must be made." *Discovery and the Capitalist Process* (Chicago: University of Chicago Press, 1985), 17. Samuel Gregg comments incisively on Kirzner's statement: "'Assessment' is the key word here. It highlights the reality that each person's knowledge is limited and that each individual's acts consequently take place in, and contribute to, a context of uncertainty. For if there were no uncertainty, decision making would merely call for the precise calculation of facts and options, in which case, humans would be nothing more than robots. The reality is, however, that no matter how accurate one's calculations, a decision will be poor if its entrepreneurial-speculative component involves poor judgment." "The Rediscovery

of Entrepreneurship: Developments in the Catholic Tradition," in *Christianity and Entrepreneurship: Protestant and Catholic Thoughts* (Australia: Center for Independent Studies, 1999), 65.

33. Monasteries were originally conceived to be a refuge from worldly concerns and a place where spiritual matters dominated daily life. Medieval monasteries were regulated by a constitution or set of internal rules, which, among other things, required that vows of chastity, poverty, and obedience be taken by the monks. One of the most widespread constitutions was the Rule of Saint Benedict, which applied to both the Benedictine and Cistercian Orders. This rule set forth specific guidelines that controlled the organization and operation of monasteries and regulated the daily activities of the monks. For a recent translation with an excellent introduction and explanatory notes, see *The Rule of Saint Benedict*, trans. Anthony C. Meisel and M. L. del Mastro (Garden City: Image Books, 1975).

34. Robert B. Ekelund, Jr., Robert F. Hébert, Robert D. Tollison, Gary M. Anderson, and Audrey B. Davidson, *Sacred Trust: The Medieval Church As an Economic Firm* (New York: Oxford University Press, 1996), 53–54.

35. The Second Vatican Council's Decree on the Apostolate of Lay People (November 18, 1965) expands this argument in the following lengthy quotation:

> That men, working in harmony, should renew the temporal order and make it increasingly more perfect: Such is God's design for the world.
>
> All that goes to make up the temporal order: personal and family values, culture, economic interests, the trades and professions, institutions of the political community, international relations, and so on, as well as their gradual development—all these are not merely helps to man's last end; they possess a value of their own, placed in them by God, whether considered individually or as parts of the integral temporal structure: "And God saw all that he had made and found it very good" (Gen. 1:31). This natural goodness of theirs receives an added dignity from their relation with the human person, for whose use they have

been created. And then, too, God has willed to gather together all that was natural, all that was supernatural, into a single whole in Christ, "so that in everything he would have the primacy" (Col. 1:18). Far from depriving the temporal order of its autonomy, of its specific ends, of its own laws and resources, or its importance for human well-being, this design, on the contrary, increases its energy and excellence, raising it at the same time to the level of man's integral vocation here below (no. 7).

About the Authors

Kris Mauren is president and co-founder of the Acton Institute, an international educational think tank based in Grand Rapids, Michigan, with offices in Rome, Italy, and Buenos Aires, Argentina. The Acton Institute publishes scholarship, produces films, and organizes educational seminars around the world promoting an understanding of the ethical dimensions of the free market economy. Kris serves as a trustee for a number of institutions, including Donors Capital Fund and the John Templeton Foundation. In the past, he also served on the board of the Foundation for Economic Education. He is widely recognized as a leader in nonprofit management, consulting regularly on best practices in governance, management, measurement, and fundraising in the not-for-profit sector.

Rev. Robert A. Sirico is president emeritus and co-founder of the Acton Institute and the pastor emeritus at Sacred Heart of Jesus Parish, both in Grand Rapids, Michigan. As a regular writer and commentator on religious, political, economic, and social issues, Rev. Sirico has contributed to the *New York Times*, *Wall Street Journal*, *Forbes*, *Washington Times*, CNN, ABC, CBS, NPR, and the BBC, among others. In his book, *Defending* *the Free Market: The Moral Case for a Free Economy*, Rev. Sirico shows how a free economy is not only the best way to meet society's material needs but also the surest protection of human dignity against government encroachment. Rev. Sirico holds dual American and Italian citizenship.

The Acton Institute's Mission Statement

The Acton Institute is a think tank whose mission is to promote a free and virtuous society characterized by individual liberty and sustained by religious principles.

The Acton Institute's Core Principles

Dignity of the Person—The human person, created in the image of God, is individually unique, rational, the subject of moral agency, and a co-creator. Accordingly, he possesses intrinsic value and dignity, implying certain rights and duties for both himself and other persons. These truths about the dignity of the human person are known through revelation, but they are also discernible through reason.

Social Nature of the Person—Although persons find ultimate fulfillment only in communion with God, one essential aspect of the development of persons is our social nature and capacity to act for disinterested ends. The person is fulfilled by interacting with other persons and by participating in moral goods. There are voluntary relations of exchange such as market transactions that realize economic value. These transactions may give rise to moral value as well. There are also voluntary relations of mutual dependence such as promises, friendships, marriages, and the family, which are moral goods. These, too, may have other sorts of value such as religious, economic, aesthetic, and so on.

Importance of Social Institutions—Since persons are by nature social, various human persons develop social institutions. The institutions of civil society, especially the family, are the primary sources of a society's moral culture. These social institutions are neither created by nor derive their legitimacy from the state. The state must respect their autonomy and provide the support necessary to ensure the free and orderly operation of all social institutions in their respective spheres.

Human Action—Human persons are by nature acting persons. Through human action, the person can actualize his potentiality by freely choosing the moral goods that fulfill his nature.

Sin—Although human beings in their created nature are good, in their current state they are fallen and corrupted by sin. The reality of sin makes the state necessary to restrain evil. The ubiquity of sin, however, requires that the state be limited in its power and jurisdiction. The persistent reality of sin requires that we be skeptical of all utopian "solutions" to social ills such as poverty and injustice.

Rule of Law and the Subsidiary Role of Government—The government's primary responsibility is to promote the common good, that is, to maintain the rule of law and to preserve basic duties and rights. The government's role is not to usurp free actions, but to minimize those conflicts that may arise when the free actions of persons and social institutions result in competing interests. The state should exercise this responsibility according to the principle of subsidiarity. This principle has two components. First, jurisdictionally broader institutions must refrain from usurping the proper functions that should be performed by the person and institutions more immediate to him. Second, jurisdictionally broader institutions should assist individual persons and institutions more immediate to the person only when the latter cannot fulfill their proper functions.

Creation of Wealth—Material impoverishment undermines the conditions that allow humans to flourish. The best means of reducing poverty is to protect private property rights through the rule of law. This allows people to enter into voluntary exchange circles in which to express their creative nature. Wealth is created when human beings creatively transform matter into resources. Because human beings can create wealth, economic exchange need not be a zero-sum game.

Economic Liberty—Liberty, in a positive sense, is achieved by fulfilling one's nature as a person by freely choosing to do what one ought. Economic liberty is a species of liberty so-stated. As such, the bearer of economic liberty not only has certain rights, but also duties. An economically free person, for example, must be free to enter the market voluntarily. Hence, those who have the power to interfere with the market are duty bound to remove any artificial barrier to entry in the market, and also to protect private and shared property rights. But the economically free person will also bear the duty to others to participate in the market as a moral agent and in accordance with moral goods. Therefore, the law must guarantee private property rights and voluntary exchange.

Economic Value—In economic theory, economic value is subjective because its existence depends on it being felt by a subject. Economic value is the significance that a subject attaches to a thing whenever he perceives a causal connection between this thing and the satisfaction of a present, urgent want. The subject may be wrong in his value judgment by attributing value to a thing that will not or cannot satisfy his present, urgent want. The truth of economic value judgments is settled just in case that thing can satisfy the expected want. While this does not imply the realization of any other sort of value, something can have both subjective economic value and objective moral value.

Priority of Culture—Liberty flourishes in a society supported by a moral culture that embraces the truth about the transcendent origin and destiny of the human person. This moral culture leads to harmony and to the proper ordering of society. While the various institutions within the political, economic, and other spheres are important, the family is the primary inculcator of the moral culture in a society.